TUPI

COLORING & ACTIVITY BOOK

SEARLSTUDIO KIDS

Copyright © 2014 by Stephan Earl. All rights reserved. Internal coloring and activity pages designed and created by Katie Earl. Cover design by Stephan Earl. Illustrations by Designgraf. Based on the SearlStudio Kids book *Tupi Finds His Tune* written by Stephan Earl, illustrated by Peter Mahr. Published in the United States by SearlStudio Kids, an imprint of SearlStudio Publishing. All rights reserved. No part of this book may be reproduced, scanned, or distributed without permission in writing from its publisher, SearlStudio Publishing. Please do not participate in or encourage piracy of copyrighted materials in violation of the author's rights. Purchase only authorized editions. Printed in the United States of America.

ISBN: 978-0-9895062-5-0

www.SearlStudioKids.com

Introducing TUPI

Te presento a Tupi

One day, Tupi the toucan awakes
from his afternoon nap.
He hears music, and remembers…

Un día, Tupi, el tucán,
despierta de su siesta en la tarde.
En eso oye música y recuerda…

It's carnival time! The rainforest is alive with singing and celebration.

¡Es hora del carnaval! La selva vive con los cantos y la celebración.

Tupi flies from his home in the tree hollow to join the festivities.
Swoosh!

Tupi's adventure begins...

Tupi vuela de su casa al agujero que está en el árbol para participar en el festejo.
¡Swush!

La aventura de Tupi comienza ...

Introducing
RED EYE
the Tree Frog

Te presento a Ojito Rojo la Ranita de Árbol

Introducing SCARLET
the Macaw

Te presento a Escarlata la Guacamaya

Introducing
TOCO
the Rainforest Chief

Te presento a Toco el Jefe de la Selva Tropical

Find His Tune

Tupi needs your help to find his tune.
Tupi necesita que lo ayudes a encontrar su melodía.

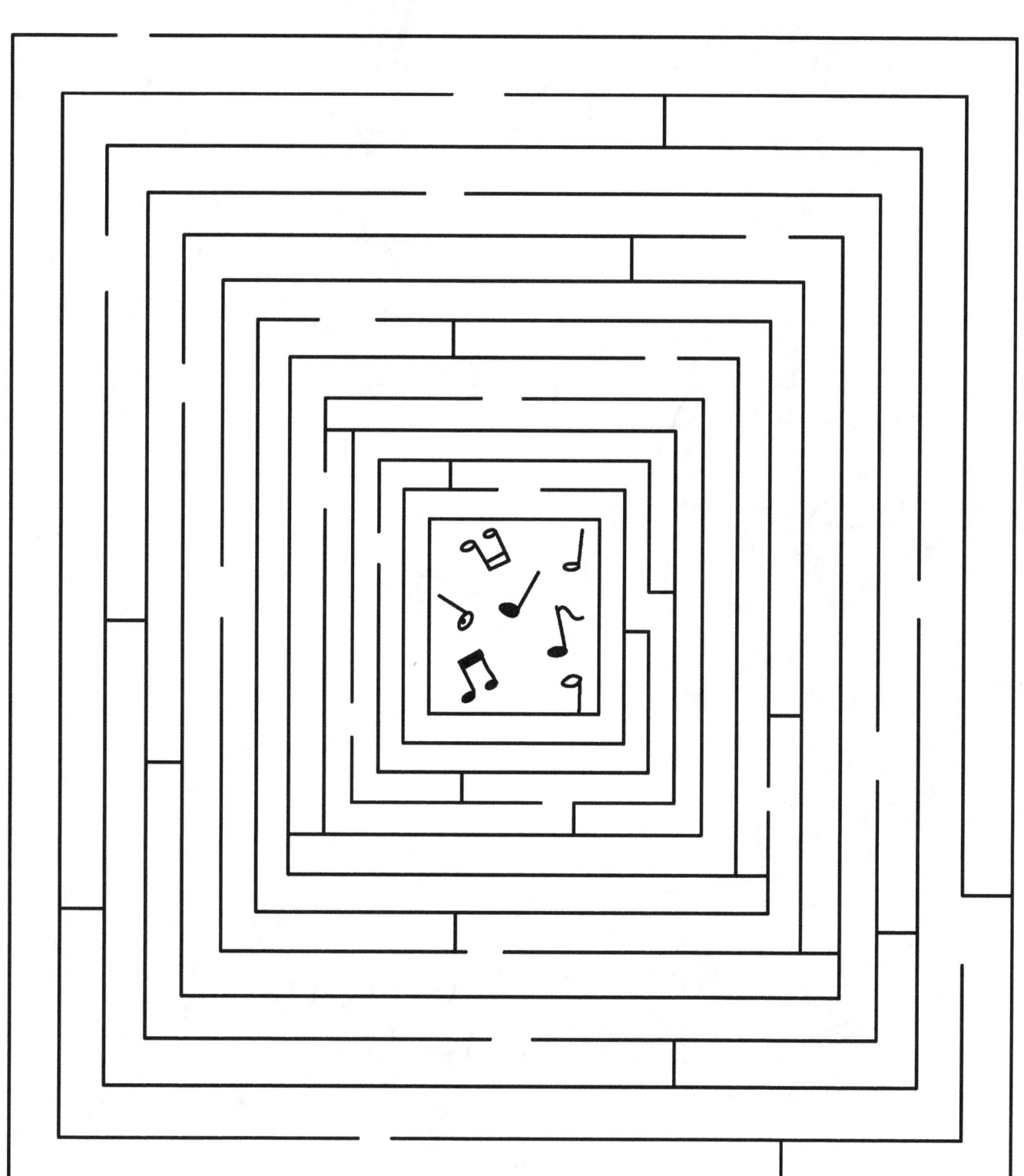

Long Beaks, Short Beaks

Put the beaks in order from longest to shortest beginning with the longest as number one.

Pon los picos en orden comenzando con el más largo al más corto el más largo es el número uno.

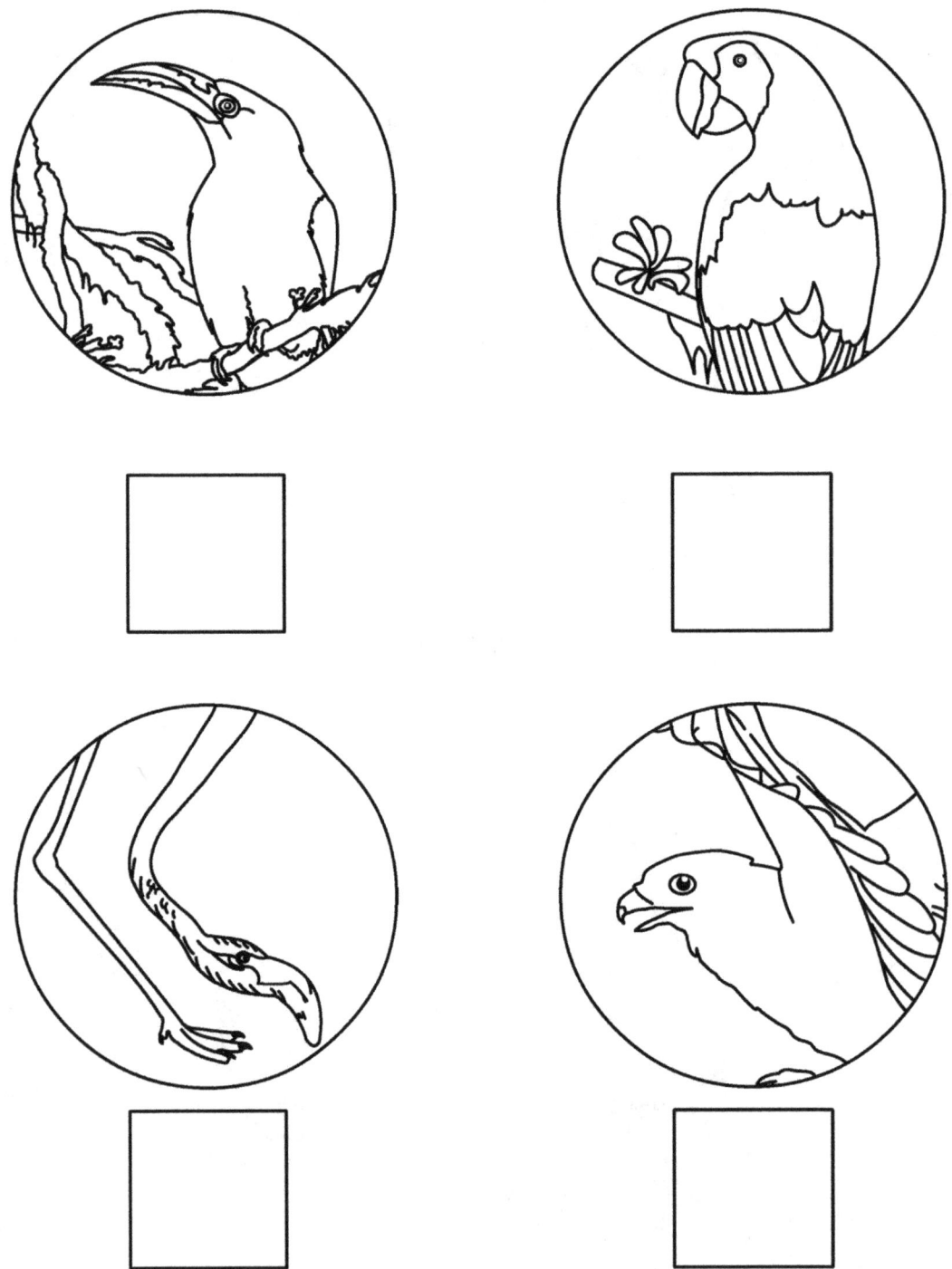

Answer key on page 60.

16

Save the Rainforest

Design a flyer to post to help keep the rainforest clean.
Diseña un volante para que lo puedas colocar en varios lugares y ayudes a mantener la selva limpia.

Mother & Baby

Draw a line to connect the baby animal with it's mother.
Dibuja una línea para que conectes al animal bebé con su madre.

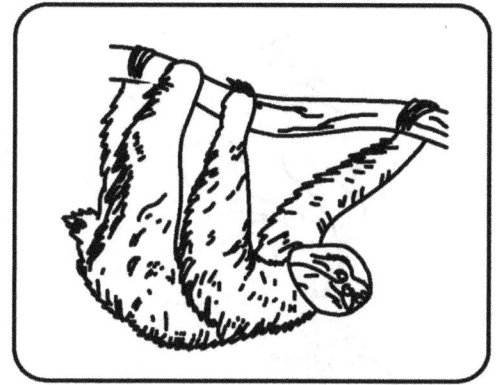

Answer key on page 60.

21

Find the Match

Mark the box of the bird that looks just like Tupi.
Marca el cajón del pájaro que es idéntico a Tupi.

Tupi starts with a "T"

How many words can you spell that start with the letter "T"?
¿Cuántas palabras puedes deletrear que comiencen con la letra "T"?

_____   _____

_____   _____

_____   _____

_____   _____

_____   _____

_____

Rainforest Word Search

Find the words in the puzzle below and circle them.
Encuentra las palabras en el juego que viene abajo y enciérralas en un círculo.

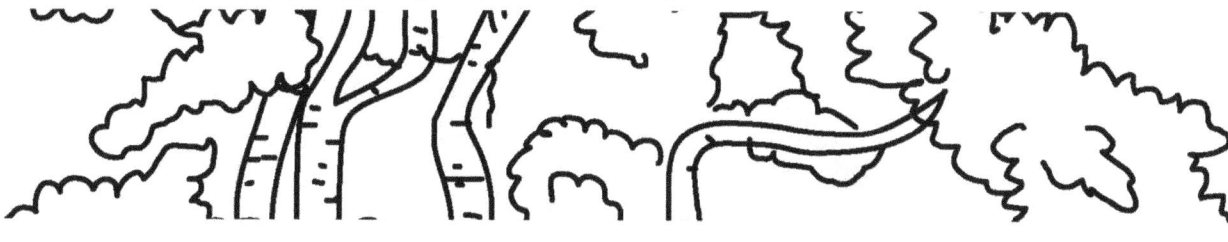

```
T O U C A N D S C
S L O T H Y T W T
F L U E E N D E R
R W F K A T I K E
O I N B U N D A E
G O X I E L A N D
M A G T I M E S C
```

MONKEY   SNAKE

FROG   TOUCAN

SLOTH   TREE

Answer key on page 61.

Count the Butterflies

Count the butterflies and write the number inside the box below.
Cuenta las mariposas y escribe el número dentro del cajón que viene abajo.

Answer key on page 61.

Color by Number

Color Tupi using the color key below.
Colorea a Tupi usando la llave que está abajo.

1 - Black   2- Dark Blue   3- Green   4- Red   5- Light Blue
1 - Negro   2- Azul Marino   3- Verde   4- Rojo   5- Azul Pastel

Count the Frogs

How many frogs do you see in the tree? Write the number in the box.
¿Cuántas ranas ves en el árbol? Escribe el número en el cajón.

Answer key on page 61.

33

Match the Instruments

Can you find the matching pair of instruments? Draw a line to connect them.
¿Puedes encontrar el par de instrumentos que concuerdan? Traza una línea para que los conectes.

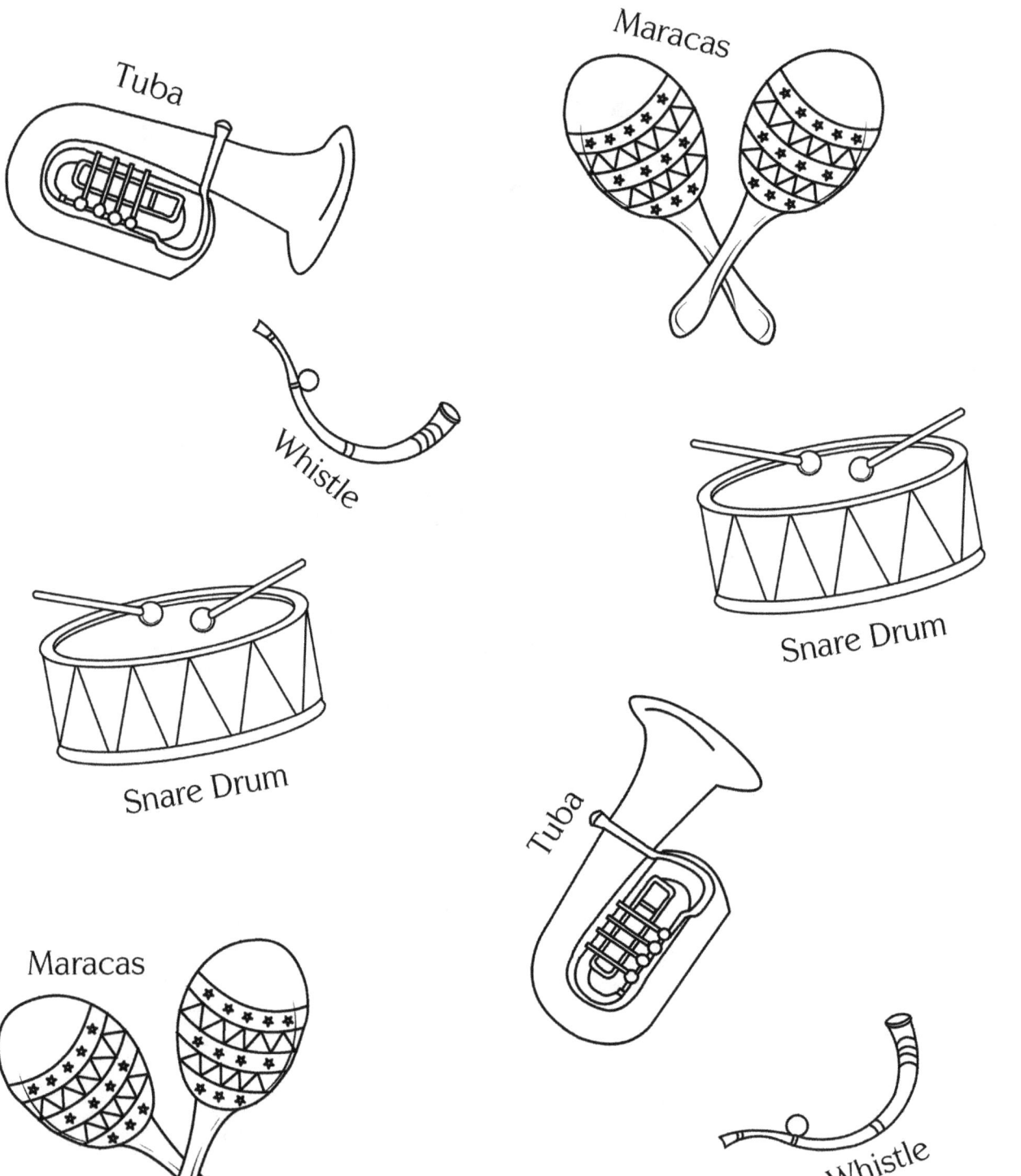

Find the Hidden Snake

Color the hidden snake.
Colorea la víbora que está escondida.

35

Flying Insects

Mark an "X" in the box of the insects that fly.
Marca con una "X" el cajón de los insectos que vuelan.

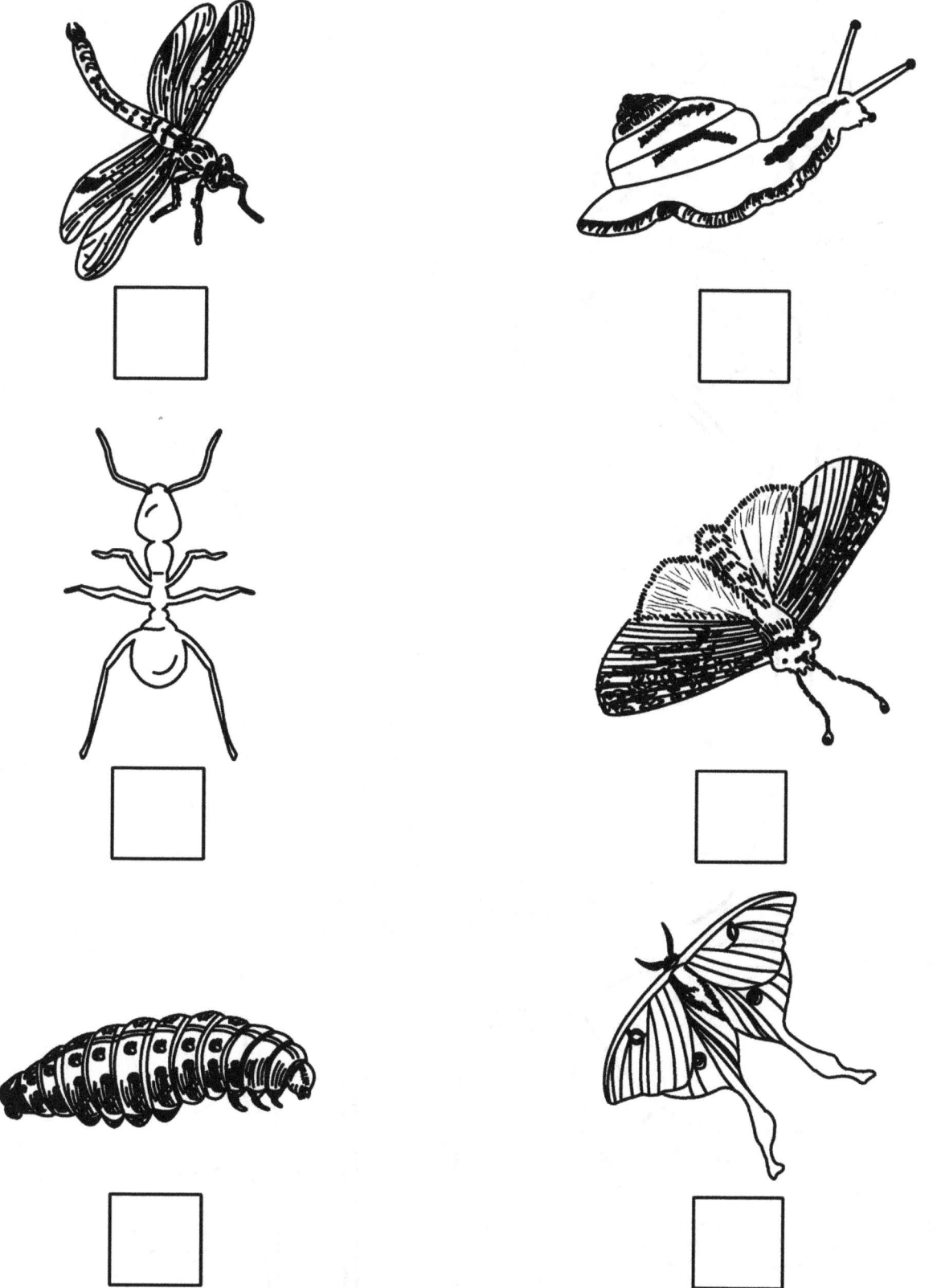

Answer key on page 62.

37

Name the Fruit

What fruit is growing on the tree? Write your answer in the boxes below.
¿Cuál fruta está creciendo en el árbol?
Escribe tu respuesta en los cajones abajo.

☐☐☐☐☐☐ tree

Celebrate Carnival Time!

Using the image on the left page finish drawing his carnival costume.
Usando la imagen que viene en la página izquierda termina de dibujar su disfraz para el carnaval.

Celebrate Carnival Time!

Using the image on the left page finish drawing her carnival costume.
Usando la imagen que viene en la página izquierda terminar de dibujar su disfraz para el carnaval.

NAME THAT INSTRUMENT?

Circle the correct intrument that each animal is playing.
Encierra en un círculo el instrumento correcto
que cada animal está tocando.

A. FLUTE or B. BASS DRUM
flauta o bombo

A. WHISTLE or B. TROMBONE
silbato o trombón

A. TRUMPET or B. GUITAR
trompeta o guitarra

A. TUBA or B. MARACAS
tuba o maracas

NAME THAT INSTRUMENT?

Circle the correct intrument that each animal is playing.
Encierra en un círculo el instrumento correcto
que cada animal está tocando.

A. SNARE DRUM or B. PIANO
tarola o piano

A. CLARINET or B. TUBA
clarinete o tuba

A. WHISTLE or B. SAXOPHONE
silbato o saxofón

Find the Bird

What item can help you see the bird high in the tree? Circle the item below.
Encierra en un círculo el objeto que viene abajo que te ayudará
a ver el pájaro desde lo alto del árbol.

Connect the Dots

Connect the dots in alphabetical order to complete Toco.
Conecta los puntos en orden alfabético para que termines a Toco.

Answer key on page 63.

Fruits!

Below are examples of fruits that grow on trees in the rainforest.
Abajo hay ejemplos de frutas que crecen
en los árboles en la selva tropical.

Mango

Lemon
limón

Papaya

Trace a Butterfly

Practice drawing the right side of the butterfly.
Practica dibujar el lado derecho de la mariposa.

Draw a Butterfly

Now that you have practiced, try to finish drawing the butterfly.
Ahora que ya has practicado, trata de terminar de dibujar la mariposa.

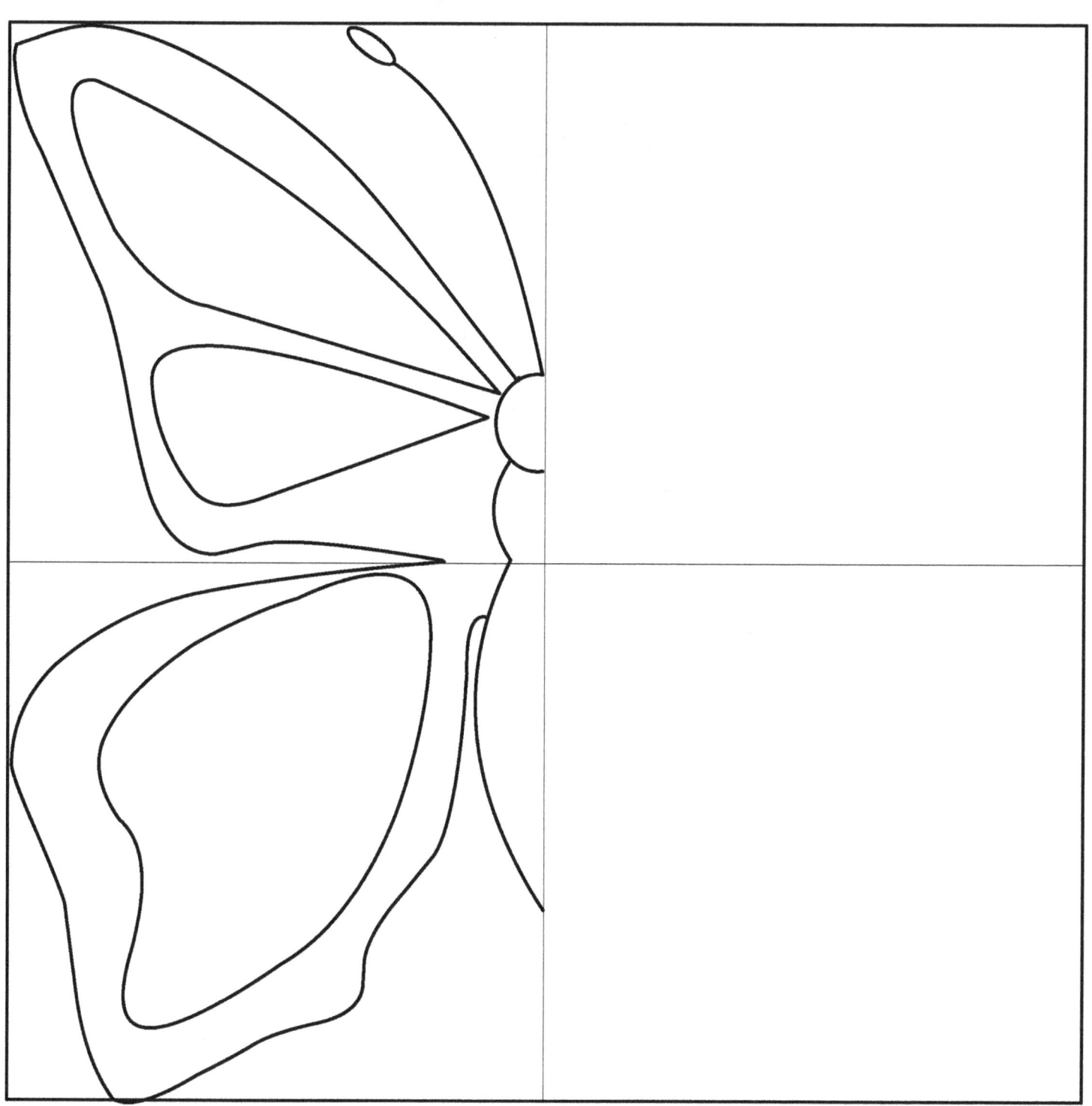

Going Camping!

Circle the item you will not need when camping.
Encierra en un círculo el objeto que NO necesitas
para ir de campamento.

Canteen
Cantimplora

Tent
Tienda de Campaña

Blanket
Cobija

Thermos
Termo

Tires
Llantas

Clock
Reloj

Answer Key

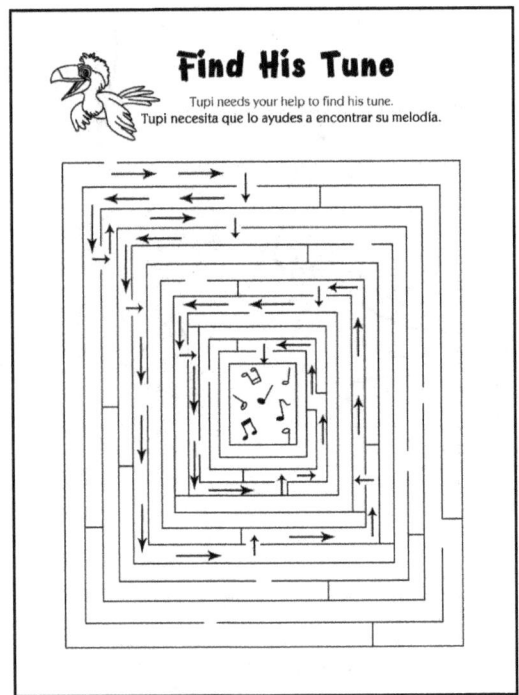

Page 13

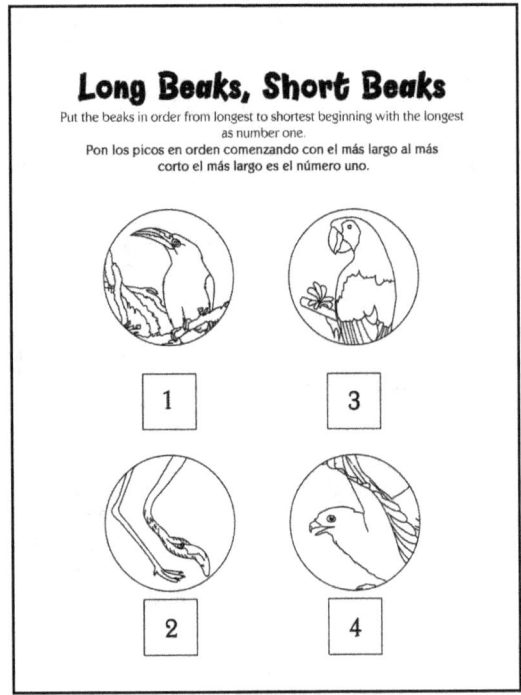

Page 16

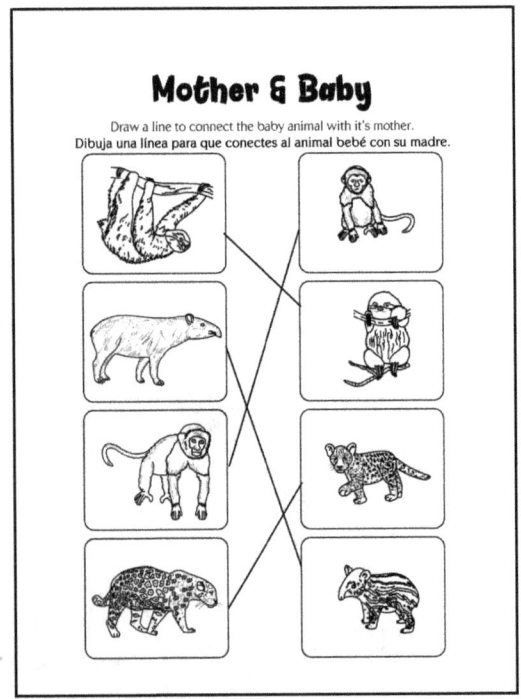

Page 21

Page 22

Answer Key

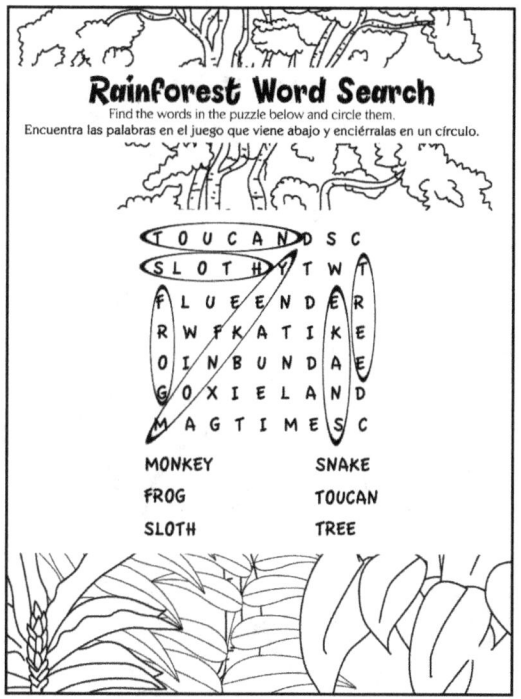

Page 27

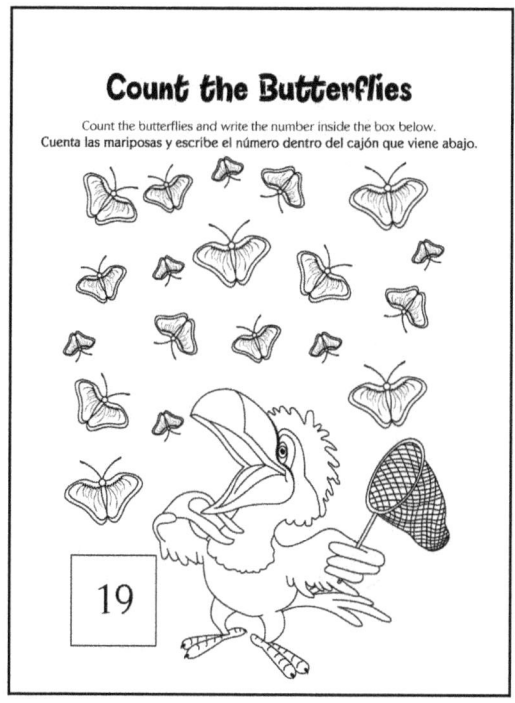

Page 29

Page 33

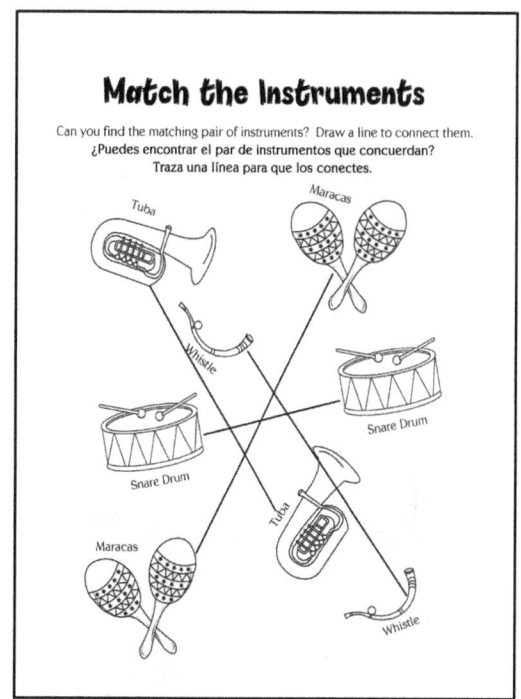

Page 34

61

Answer Key

Page 37

Page 38

Page 39

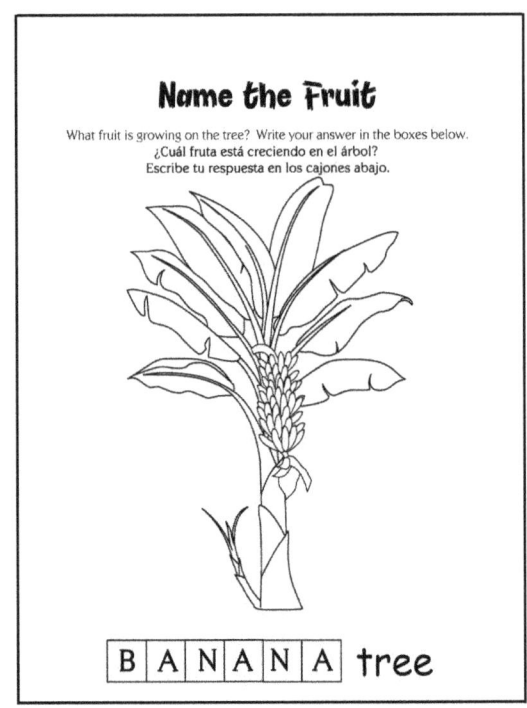

Page 42

Answer Key

Page 48

Page 49

Page 51

Page 52

Answer Key

Page 56

www.ingramcontent.com/pod-product-compliance
Lightning Source LLC
Chambersburg PA
CBHW081021040426
42444CB00014B/3303